Praise for *Sit Your*

This new book shows influencers and leaders how to ꜱoꜱ... ꜱn themselves for success in their next meeting. Whether it is a board meeting, sales presentation or public speaking event., you will learn the strategies from how to set up the room to where to best position yourself for the highest influence. LeAnn's practical and insightful, and informative approach provides every leader their guide to success. I know I won't view any meeting the same again.

Roberto Candelaria, Influencer Income Strategist
www.robertocandelaria.com

Sit Your Way to Success is a perfect guide for any entrepreneur or business owner who is looking for key success strategies in their business. This book is your guide to reach your desired result for every meeting. The strategies LeAnn shares will reframe your thinking and plans in your meetings and sales presentations.

Bill Walsh, America's Small Business Expert
www.ipowerteam.com

"Who would think that seating position matters this much? LeAnn would, and she explains this and more in *Sit Your Way to Success*. In clear, concise language, she shares the facts and explains the psychology behind these truths. Step by step, she leads you through several types of meetings and how to maximize results just by giving some extra thought to where to position the attendees. An easy, quick but meaningful read full of powerful information you can use immediately."

Jim Malkus, CEO & President, www.indoff.com

Sit Your Way to Success is a must-read for all. I will never look at a table the same way. I was surprised with how much research LeAnn provided about seating and table shapes. As a regular "attendee" of meetings, I'm paying more attention to how seating choices impact the conversation and flow of meetings. Thank you for this business success "hack".

Angel Tuccy, Author & Speaker
www.MakeYourBigImpact.com

Sit Your Way to Success is a must-read for any leader, trainer, consultant, salesperson, and even host/hostess! While some of this may be intuitive, especially for those of us who have been around for a while, it's the nuances we don't know that could significantly impact the outcome of a meeting or event. I'm either going to memorize the book, or make sure I consult it before every important sales meeting and presentation - or both!!!

Dawn Shuler, CEO, www.TheShulerGroupLLC.com

SIT YOUR WAY TO
SUCCESS

From Sales Meetings
to Dinner Parties,
Where You Sit Matters!

LeAnn Pashina

Special discounts are available for quantity purchases. For details, email info@creativelycommunicate.com

Published by:
CC Ink Press
www.CCInkPress.com

Cover design by: LeAnn Pashina and Naeem Khan

Interior Layout by: B Qureshi

All diagrams, drawings and graphs by LeAnn Pashina

Sit Your Way to Success: From Sales Meetings to Dinner Parties, Where You Sit Matters

ISBN 978-1-7337887-0-0

First Edition

Printed in the United States of America

TABLE OF
CONTENTS

Introduction

This book will benefit you if you are in sales, conduct or participate in meetings, attend trainings, or present to an audience.

Most meetings and interactions take place when we are seated at a table, an event, or presentation. Where you sit in relation to others in these meetings influences the outcome, yet most of us don't consciously make a calculated choice.

Being in corporate sales for over 30 years, I've attended hundreds of meetings, most of which included a table or desk of some type. In the beginning of my career, I would randomly select a seat, typically the one closest to the door or where my client would suggest, not knowing at the time that utilizing the right seating arrangement could help in closing the sale.

I hadn't stopped to think about seating arrangements specifically until I came across some research on the psychology of learning as it applies to room layouts. The more I discovered, the clearer it became that where one sits has an impact on the result of the meeting. I thought about all my past meetings, and the ones that were most successful were typically at a small meeting table where the meeting seemed more relaxed, the conversation flowed easily, and the sale seemed to come naturally.

During my 30-year career selling furniture to companies of all sizes, I have designed and installed conference and /or meeting rooms in almost every facility. Designing the layout of the space includes specifying the shape of the table or desk and how it's situated in the room. In my early years as a trained Interior Designer, my approach was functional and aesthetic. Gradually, I began to understand the psychology of seating arrangements, and am now able to incorporate this invaluable information in my designs.

With this book, you will understand where and why you choose your seat and that choosing the right seat helps you reach your intended goal, whether it's to close a sale, lead a meeting, teach others, or have a great conversation. The simple act of taking a seat at the table can predetermine your outcome.

The research and information I share are compiled and organized to be used as a reference book. You can pick it up and easily understand the information and begin to apply it in both your personal life and your professional life.

The various drawings and illustrations of table shapes, as well as room and office layouts, will help you easily visualize the content. Of course, you can read all the information in detail, and each chapter also has a summary section, which provides quick access to the content, and helps you find the key resources easily.

Whether you are new to sales or have been around for a while like me, you will discover lots of tips that you can apply immediately. If you conduct meetings, train, or teach others, this new seating paradigm will yield more effective results.

My goal is to offer insights into seat selection for any situation. Enjoy all the "a-ha" moments and discoveries as you move your way through the book. I warn you; you won't look at any meeting in the same way again.

So, pull up a seat and let's begin!!

Chapter One

Overview and History

The first major research studies completed in the area of seating arrangements were done in the late 1960's by environmental psychologist Robert Sommer. The research revealed that where we sit in a meeting greatly affects several things.

- Other participants' perceptions of us
- Feelings toward others and feelings toward what is being discussed in the meeting
- The status of relationships to others in the room
- Whether one feels included or excluded in the meeting

Since that first study, there have been several other research studies conducted to further discover the effect of seating arrangements in the classroom and learning environments, conference meetings, sales meetings, dining experiences, as well as how as how those seating arrangements affect relationships and conversations. In many situations, humans are predictable in their behavior as it relates to seating arrangements, these studies helped us to better understand that behavior.

Our understanding of this behavior will guide us in conducting more productive meetings; increased collaboration and interaction among participants; and improve learning and subject retention among students and the audience. The information is not intended to use to manipulate the environment in a negative or selfish directive, but instead to create more effective results.

When we make our seat selection
we send messages about ourselves
to the other members of the group

When we make our seat selection, we send messages about ourselves to the other members of the group. The opinions or judgments made by others are not random and provide insight into the power dynamics in a room or meeting. Observing another person's seating choice, just like observing their body language, reveals various insights such as motives, relationship to others, and personality traits, to name a few. When we understand these various dynamics, we can actively utilize the information to achieve our goals.

History

Throughout history, and especially in medieval times, where you sat at the table defined your relative importance and nobility. Arguments would erupt over who belonged where at the table, which at times would result in sword fights. This led to using name placards for formal dinners to prevent arguments and squabbles. This quickly revealed the importance and position of each person at the table, whether a social dinner party or a business meeting. If you lost favor with the host, your seat position would reveal it.

When kings sat on their thrones with their retinue around them, everyone knew the status and position of everyone. It was reflected in their relative proximity to the king and on which side they sat. This arrangement served a king or leader well in a dictatorship environment, but not if collaboration and a democratic procedure was desired.

Most of us are familiar with King Arthur and the Knights of the Round Table. The table was first mentioned in about 1155, in Wace's *Roman de Brut*. Wace explains that the King installed the table in order to prevent quarrels over seating precedence, as a circular table had no head and created an environment where all had equal status and positions at the table.

Unfortunately, this logical plan was not always achieved, for other historical writings state how there had been brawls at the court over seating positions. In addition, the actual size of the table is highly disputed. The number of knights around the table varied from 12 to 25 or more. Anything over 25 around one table would be quite unwieldy.

One well-known table was the Winchester Round Table, 18 feet in diameter and could sit 25 people. Now that is one large table! And it proved to counter the original intent of everyone being of equal status. One can imagine that if the table was 18 feet across, then the proximity to the King had meaning of one's status. The closer a knight was to the King, the more an unspoken higher rank was assumed. And the person sitting next to the King would have his "ear" and have influence on the discussion.

As much as we don't want to show preferential treatment in many situations, perception is not always our friend. The information in the following chapters will explore the various dynamics that exist when it applied to seating arrangements in various settings. The information is based on research and observations, and I'll provide more references in the appropriate chapters (and in the reference section at the end).

You will be able to utilize this information to apply to your next meeting or event to achieve your purpose. Human nature is not predictable 100 percent of the time, so I can't guarantee the same results in every instance, although statistically speaking, this information is true in most situations.

That being said, why not give yourself a leg up by consciously choosing where to sit? By simply deciding where you will sit in a room, you will influence others and potentially affect the outcome of the meeting.

When you have completed this book, I promise you will see seating arrangements differently. You will have insight in every situation you are in and every seat available to you.

Chapter Two

Table Shapes

Tables are available in a wide variety of shapes and sizes. History shows us that tables were either a rectangle, square, or round. Nothing really changed until relatively recently. When I began my interior design career in the early 1980's, this was still the case more often than not. I may have seen a unique shape here or there, although they were generally custom-made and not readily available to all. The standard approach in deciding which table shape to use largely depended upon the size of the room, not how the room would be used.

During the past several years, how a room will be used has become as important as table shape. Choosing which shape and size is best for you and the outcomes you seek can be overwhelming. The furniture industry (mainly contract or corporate, not residential) has been responsive to changes within the business world, technology advances and how those affect the office environment, as well as changes within corporate culture. Historically, if you wanted a uniquely shaped table, you would need to have it designed and custom built. Now, there is so much variety that it is easy to find a manufacturer who offers uniquely-shaped tables in their standard line.

Before we get into where to sit, let's start with table shape. To determine which shape is best for your space and needs, begin by answering the following questions to establish the optimal design.

- How will the room be used? For general meetings, training, or both?
- What meeting type or style is preferred: formal or informal? Formal boardroom style where one person leads and controls the meeting? Or one in which there will be collaboration among the participants?
- Will there be a designated leader?
- What is the desired degree of individual involvement and interaction?
- Will technology be utilized during meetings, such as video or audio conferencing, screen or monitor use for presentations, and Internet access?
- Will the room be used in several formats as of a multi-purpose room?

Your answers will help you to determine which table shape will work best for your meeting purpose. The size of the room will determine the size of the table. You will find charts illustrating how many chairs fit around each table, shape, and size for easy reference in the resource section.

This chapter provides an overview of most of the table shapes available in the marketplace. There may be some slight variations of each that won't be addressed, although the basic information is helpful when deciding which is best for you. We'll review each shape and provide a summary of each shape to assist you in your selection.

In later chapters where we discuss positions and seating arrangements, you will want to incorporate the information on various table shapes discussed in this chapter.

(With any of these tables, there is the ability to add electrical and data plugs. There is such a variety of grommets and accessories available that it is easy to customize to specific needs.)

Rectangle shape:

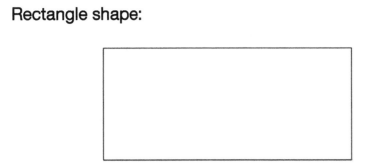

Diagram 1

Rectangle is the standard shape table which has been around for ages. It has two short ends and two long sides. The ends are typically the "head of the table" and used for the leader of the meeting. This shape breeds a general mood of competition and confrontation, since most people will sit opposite to one another with the table as a barrier between them. The shape does not encourage a spirit of cooperation; however, the shape does function well in the business world where one dominant individual controls the flow of the meeting, and everyone looks to this individual to make the final decision(s).

In the following chapter on positions, you will learn how the other sections of the table can be used best in any meeting.

This table is available in just about any length, and it typically starts at 36" wide for the shorter lengths, and then goes to 42"wide, with the most common being the 48" width by whatever length. Once the table is very long, 30 feet and more, you will often see the width increase to 60 inches, mainly for perspective, so the table doesn't appear so long in a room.

Advantages:

- Style can fit into any décor, from traditional to contemporary
- Fits easily in a standard rectangular room
- Variety of sizes available

Purpose:

- Standard boardroom and conference meetings
- Formal meetings

Boat shape:

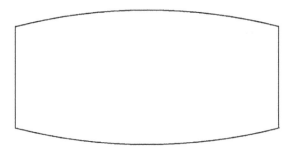

Diagram 2

This table is called Boat shape, as it resembles the shape of a typical boat that expands outward in the middle; essentially, it is a modification of a standard rectangle. This table shape has been around for a while and will typically have more of a traditional style in the table edge details and support bases than the simple, clean details of a contemporary style. If the room allows this shape, it is a visually appealing alternative to the rectangle. The outward-bowed sides allow the people sitting around the table to better see one another. You won't have to look around another person's head to be able to see who is talking, as you do with the rectangular table.

This table is available in just about any length, although you really can't appreciate the shape until you are at an eight-foot length or more. The bow of the center is determined by, and in proportion to the length of the table. For example, a six-foot-long table will have just a slight bow to it; otherwise the proportion would make the table look rather odd. So, preferable sizes with this shape are either a 10-foot-long where each end would be at 36 inches and the center bows out to 48 inches wide; or a 12-foot-long where the ends are at 42 inches and the center bows out to 54 inches wide.

Advantages:

- Style is more traditional
- Fits easily in standard rectangular room
- Helps to provide better eye contact between people sitting at the table
- Variety of sizes available

Purpose:

- Standard boardroom meetings
- Formal meetings

Racetrack:

Diagram 3

When looking at the drawing, you can see why it is called Racetrack, for it is the shape of a standard racetrack. This is a great shape to use in a conference room because if you have a meeting and need to fit additional people around the table, no one will have to sit at a corner as they would with a rectangular or boat-shaped table. The curved ends of this table are less restrictive and help to create a meeting environment that is less formal than the traditional shapes.

Advantages:

- Style is transitional; it falls into traditional or contemporary
- Fits easily in standard rectangular room
- No corners
- Variety of sizes available

Purpose:

- Standard boardroom meetings
- Good for standard meetings that are more business casual, rather than formal

Oval:

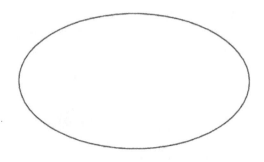

Diagram 4

The Oval shape is a combination between the racetrack and boat shape. It creates a more collaborative and friendlier environment. There is a head of the table, yet it is not as distinct as with prior shapes, because the seats are closer to one another. In addition, it helps to establish a more equal status among participants, as you find with the round shape. This shape also works well in private offices. Depending upon the size of the office and furniture needs, this often fits better than a standard round table because more people can fit around it.

Advantages:

- Style is transitional and contemporary
- Fits easily in standard rectangular room and office
- No corners
- Variety of sizes available. This shape will vary quickly depending upon the width and length ratio desired

Purpose:

- Good for standard meetings that are more business casual
- Creates more collaboration among members
- Good shape to use when a round table is too small

Square:

Diagram 5

The Square shape is usually reserved for relaxed, comfortable, and informal conversations. You will often see this kind of table in dining rooms, cafeterias, coffee shops, and restaurants. You can also push two tables together to create a rectangle and provide additional seating. It provides flexibility regarding positions, as you will learn in the next chapter regarding competitive and cooperative positions. When four people are sitting at the table, everyone is equally competing and cooperating which aids in leveling the playing field. This is also a great shape for quick, serious, and to-the-point meetings in the business world. There isn't a significant single power position with this table shape.

Square tables are also good in offices for more casual meetings, and they can be easily pushed flush against the wall if space is limited.

Advantages:

- Style will fit into any decorative scheme or setting
- Every place at the table has equal positioning to the others
- Ability to push two together to create a rectangle - provides flexibility

Purpose:

- Creates equal positioning among participants
- Relaxed, comfortable conversations
- If two people are meeting, one individual can assume a formal, defensive position, or one can choose to sit in a corner position to create a more co-operative, intimate encounter
- Informal meetings

Round:

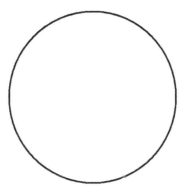

Diagram 6

The Round shape creates an atmosphere of relaxed informality and is ideal for promoting discussions, because everyone is of equal status, as each person can claim the same amount of table territory. Therefore, everyone has an equal amount of authority and status (as long as one of them is not the King).

The diameter of the table is important to consider depending upon its use. The smaller the diameter, the more intimate the meeting.

Small round tables with 24- to 30-inch diameters are often in bars and restaurants for intimate dining and conversations because only two or three people can sit comfortably at the table. Standard 36"- and 48"-diameter tables are also used in typical dining areas and restaurants and accommodate four people comfortably. Tables with diameters of 60" or greater are used in larger banquet settings, which is helps to inspire conversation and collaboration.

In business facilities, round tables are usually a place to relax and converse or to drink coffee. Round tables can reduce pressure and build trust. Companies use these areas to build alliances with potential clients, (especially timid ones), break down barriers, and create rapport. Also, they are promoting team-oriented discussions and eliminate the need to speak over a desk.

Advantages:

- Variety of sizes available
- Fits into any style
- Facilitates both intimate and large group discussions, depending upon table size

Purpose:

- Generates peaceful and cooperative discussions – everyone feels equally involved
- Promotes brainstorming; it encourages a free flow of ideas by everyone
- Creates a relaxed atmosphere during employee interviews or reviews.
- Informal meetings

The most famous example for this table shape is the Round Table of King Arthur. Before the round table, a medieval king usually sat at one end of the table, with the court jester facing him at the other end. The knights were seated at the two sides with the most important among them seated closer to the king. King Arthur attempted to equalize authority and status amongst his knights with the round table. He felt that by eliminating the "head of the table" position, his knights would see themselves as equal peers, thereby preventing quarrels.

What King Arthur failed to realize with his round table, however, was the trickle-down effect whereby those seated on his immediate left and right held the next level of power, due to their proximity to him. As one was more removed from the king, the level of status diminished, until finally reaching the most distant status. Unfortunately for this person, he faced the king, putting him in a directly competitive arrangement.

In summary, when a definitive leader is present, the round table still presents obstacles with regard to equal participation.

Research on positioning supports this with the following conclusions:

- 68% of people view the person sitting directly opposite them as the one most likely to argue or be competitive.
- 58% said that sitting opposite another could be used to show non-involvement or lack of interest, as in a public library.
- 71% said they were either having a friendly conversation or co-operating when sitting directly beside another person.

Even with all this data, it can be said that similar relationships arise with round tables as with rectangular tables. When people wish to cooperate, they sit side-by-side; when they wish to be independent, they keep one space open between each party; and when they wish to compete, they sit at opposite sides.

When it is desirable to maintain flow between three people equally, it is best to use a triangular sitting position at a round table, which encourages discussion amongst all members. In addition, this particular seating arrangement allows eye contact between all members and discourages creation of rank and power.

V-Shape:

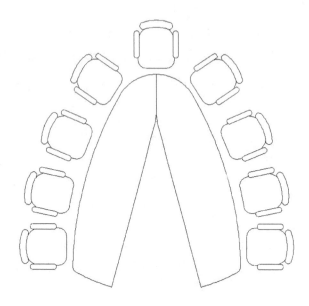

Diagram 7

The V-Shape table was designed more for video conferencing. The design basically takes a rectangular table and splits it down the center lengthwise and then pulls it apart to create a "V" shape.

In a video conferencing situation, when the monitor is at the widest end, the camera is directed toward the table, and all participants can be seen by those in the virtual room. It is also advantageous for those seated at the table because they can easily see the monitor and others seated at the table. For the person leading the meeting, he or she has a prime viewing position of all participants and holds the seat at the head of the table.

Advantages:

- Available in a variety of sizes to fit most conference rooms
- There are table designs available in the market place that allow the two ends to be pushed back together to create a standard rectangle for meetings

Purpose:

- Great for video-conference meetings
- Encourages participation and collaborations in meetings because each person can see others easily

U-Shape:

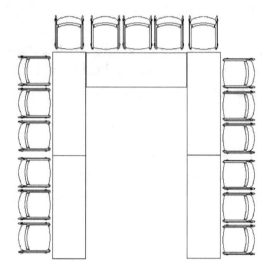

Front of Room

Diagram 8

The U-shape can be either a rounded "U," as in a horseshoe shape, or a squared "U" shape (as seen above). This shape is usually created by combining several tables, although I have seen a couple of large conference rooms with a U-shape table designed specifically for that room. This shape is ideal for larger meetings so that each participant can see every other person in the meeting. It encourages more interaction, since each person feels more a part of the meeting. The open center part can easily be modified to be wider or narrower, depending upon the room and the number of seats needed.

The U-shaped configuration also works well for presentations. The presenter is at the open end of the layout ("front of room") and can enter the open area for a more intimate connection to participants, while allowing each person can still see the presenter. This works well if one has items to show those seated at the table. It also provides a clear view for all seated at the table.

This shape layout can be easily achieved by using a modular table system or several standard rectangular tables, which will also provide flexibility for the use of the space.

Advantages:

- Style is traditional or contemporary
- Variety of sizes and layouts can be created

Purpose:

- Encourages participation and collaborations in meetings because each person can see others easily
- The open end provides a focal point and allows for a presentation area

Optional Shapes:

There are several modifications of the shapes discussed already available in the marketplace, from trapezoids, triangles, half round, pie shapes, and anything in-between. The advantage of using a modular table system is you can create any layout desired for a specific purpose. Many businesses have a multi-purpose room used for a variety of meetings and events and utilizing these different shapes increases the functionality of the room.

The following examples showcase various shapes and some configuration ideas. Each shape is a modification of the table shapes discussed previously, and depending upon how they are configured, you can refer back to the shape it resembles for details that will aid you in making calculated design/layout decisions.

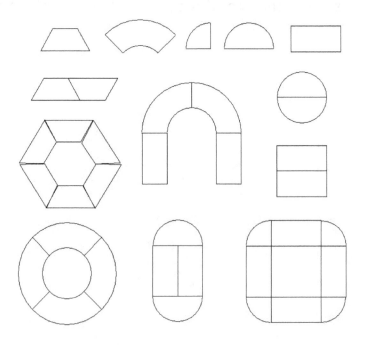

Diagram 9

Chapter Notes

When selecting a table, first determine the purpose of the meetings you will hold. The shape of the table can be an advantage to your desired outcome, or a disadvantage if not thought through carefully. Here is a quick overview of what we discussed:

For formal meetings where you want a clear leader or head of the table, the following shapes work best:

- Rectangle
- Boat shape
- Racetrack

For casual business meetings where your goal is to create a relaxed atmosphere, open to collaboration and discussion, use these shapes:

- Oval
- Square
- Round

For video conferencing, utilize these shapes:

- V-shape
- U-shape

For meetings with a "front of room" focal point and several participants where the goal is to encourage discussion, use this shape:

- U-shape

Now that you have a clear understanding of the various shapes of tables available and which shape will work best for your meeting, the following chapters will guide you in understanding how to utilize seating positions at each table.

Chapter Three

Conference Meetings

Most of us don't have a shortage of meetings to attend. If you already have a full schedule, your priority may just be to get to the meeting on time, and not even think about where you should strategically sit at the table. Yet, which seat you select at the meeting table will directly influence your effectiveness in the meeting. Your physical seat position influences how you're perceived by everyone else and, to a certain extent, predetermines the role you play. Understanding the psychology behind the various positions at a table will help you decide which seat will be best to help achieve your goal.

There is much research to support the psychology behind the various seating positions. However, I'll simply provide the highlights. The following information will provide some insights and understandings for you to utilize in your meetings.

Before we look at the details of each seat position at the table and the meaning and strategy behind it, you first want to consider your goal or purpose of the meeting. You don't always have the same purpose for every meeting you attend or lead.

If you are the boss or the one leading the meeting, one position will be better than another. Or you may intend to observe and add encouragement, so the seat you choose should support that goal. Office politics may also come into play, and if you don't know what they are, you can test where you sit to find out.

Bottom line: know your goal or purpose before you enter the room and make your seating choice.

The following questions will help you determine you goal or purpose for the meeting.

- Will you be leading the meeting?
- Do you have information and value to add to the meeting? If so, you want to be seen and heard.
- Do you want cooperation and agreement from others in the meeting?
- Is your desire to persuade others to your point of view?
- Is cooperation and agreement the desired goal, or control and persuasion?
- Do you anticipate disharmony or disagreement among the members attending? If so, you can be strategic regarding whom you sit next to in the meeting.

Each seating position has different psychological influence and meaning. But first, it's helpful to understand a few other key points about the dynamics of a typical conference room setting before diving into the details.

In any meeting, one's perception is often more influential to the outcome than the facts that exist.

> *"Perception is reality. If you are perceived to be something, you might as well be it because that's the truth in people's minds."*
>
> *Steve Young*

Proximity to others in a meeting creates connections among participants. It often denotes agreement with another's point of view. It's human nature. We think that objects that are closer together are connected and that applies to people as well. The closer you are to someone physically, the closer you feel to them. If you sit next to someone, you often are subconsciously tied to their ideas. Does someone talk too much? Don't sit near them. Is there someone who you often agree with? Sit near them! You can use proximity to your advantage in a meeting. If you know there will be discussion on a topic where there will be disagreements and opposing views, you will have more success sitting near those who have the same or similar thoughts as you do. Your point of view will be more influential than if you sat next to those who oppose your view and offer more resistance than cohesiveness.

To take proximity one step further, research shows that the influence one has by sitting to the right or left of someone will also affect the outcome. If you want your thoughts and opinions heard by the leader, sit to his or her left. If you want to show that you support and agree with the leader, sit to his or her right. This position is often the leader's biggest ally and is the literal definition of the phrase "right hand man". Sitting to the left of the leader provides you easy access to the leader for your thoughts and ideas to be heard and considered. Either of these seats are beneficial because you are next to the leader, so you have direct eye contact, which provides rapport and you're able to quickly get his or her attention. You have the advantage of being heard by the leader; essentially you have "their ear" when needed. You can whisper thoughts, ideas and key information.

Proximity in seating arrangements is one of the key factors in determining the success or failure of your participation in a meeting. Each arrangement changes the environment by changing the ways in which participants interact with the leader and with one another. Keep this in mind at your next meeting, and you can profoundly change the outcome.

After physical proximity, eye contact is one of the most powerful forms of non-verbal communication. We use eye contact as a method to control interaction and conversation. Making eye contact with other members at the table is an important key to your effectiveness. The leader of the meeting indicates his/her dominance by making and maintaining eye contact with those at the table and eye contact is just as important for the participants in a meeting as it is for the leader.

You can use seating arrangements in a meeting to diffuse opposition

If you are the meeting leader, selecting the seat at the head of the table provides you with the best overall view of each participant. Knowing this, you can use seating arrangements in a meeting to diffuse opposition. If you expect there will be some disagreements among members, you can assign seats so that those in opposition will not be directly across from one another where direct eye contact is possible and one can "stare down" their opponent. Instead, arrange to have opponents sit so they won't have direct eye contact with one another; without direct eye contact, they are less likely to stir up trouble and more likely to join in and have a reasonable discussion of the issue.

The diagram below illustrates a typical conference meeting layout. The letters noted for each seat will be referred to when discussing each position at the table. You can apply this same information to the other various table shapes. As you gain a greater understanding about seating positions, you can apply that knowledge in every meeting, no matter what variables are at play (I.e. size and shape of the room, room layout and whether or not you're simply attending or leading).

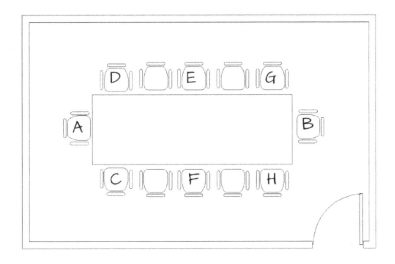

Diagram 10

Position A: The Power Position

The power position is at the head of the table. Everyone in the meeting can see you. From this seat, you can best facilitate the flow and direction of the meeting. This seat is usually reserved for the boss, or highest position in a company, or the person leading the meeting. It is referred to as the power position because it applies to the power dynamics of the meeting, not the person's ego (although you have probably experienced this in a meeting or two as well).

As the leader in the power position you have better control of the agenda and ability to keep the meeting on task and generate decisions. A meeting will lose direction and focus if there is no clear leader, so this position serves the role best. We unconsciously designate the person in this position as the one who has the most authority.

Another important aspect is the location to the door. In the diagram, position A has full view of the door. The power position will not have their back to the door, for this would diminish power and influence due to not having full view of the room and anyone who enters. This position also provides direct eye contact with everyone at the table, which also supports leadership and control of the meeting, unlike those sitting next to one another where direct eye contact is more difficult.

This position also contributes to perception of leadership. Studies focused on leadership found that the most dominant person chooses this position, and when no leader was present, the person who sits at this position is attributed as being the leader. If you don't intend or desire to be the leader, don't choose this position.

In another study, researchers Fred Strodtbeck and Harmon Hook found that during jury deliberations, people who sit in the power position tend to participate more often, and have a greater influence on the decision-making process, than the others at the table. This study did not explore whether or not the people who chose this position self-identified as a leader, but we may be able to assume that these people play the role of leader elsewhere in their lives.

Other studies have supported the conclusion that a person's status plays a part in choosing the head of the table. Those considered high class were much more likely than lower classes to self-select and sit at the head of the table (thus choosing the power position almost by default). Who knew money had anything to do with where we sit at a table?!

Select this position when you:

- are the leader or boss
- control the meeting
- desire to show authority

Position B: Second Highest

Position B, or immediately opposite the leader, is often for the person with the second-highest status in a meeting. This seat also has full view of all those at the table, providing the ability to easily add support to the leader and take note of the meeting dynamics of the participants. When two people are running a meeting, it is best if each person takes a position at each end of the table, which is a great way to show a balanced viewpoint and cohesion in leadership.

In some situations, this seat is often reserved for a guest attending the meeting. This position can facilitate slipping in and out of the meeting without causing much disturbance should he or she need to leave prior to the end of the meeting.

If you are the leader and in position A/power position, it is important to understand another potential dynamic of position B/second highest. As previously discussed in the table shape section, Position B is opposite the leader and that seat can turn into a confrontational position because it affords the person seated there an opportunity to voice disagreement with the main meeting leader in Position A/power position. In other words, if there isn't cohesion in leadership and you're the leader, you may not want to allow opposing leadership to sit in Position B.

If there is not a person who holds that second-in-command position and no one you know will support you and the agenda, it may be best to minimize the possibility of any opposition that could arise. This can be done by either removing the seat in position B or having a whiteboard or monitor on that end to prevent individuals from sitting there.

Seats C and D: Proximity to the power position

When the leader is positioned at seat A, then these flanking seats of C and D become supportive positions to the leader. Both positions have the ear of the leader and can influence the flow of the meeting by assisting the leader. The person seated to the right of the leader, seat C, will tend to be more co-operative to the leader than the person in seat D who may utilize this position to whisper influences to the leader (as discussed in the section on proximity).

While we have evolved beyond situations in which knife-play occurs, historically, the person on the right (seat C) is less likely to be able to successfully stab the leader with a knife with their left hand; hence the 'right-hand man' is more favored, and others subconsciously credit the right-hand person with having more power than the one on the left side. Research supports that most right-handed people are also right-side dominant which most often creates a preference, in the meeting leader, to looking to his or her right for support and answers. While we no longer carry knives as in medieval times, one's words can be just as "stabbing" and harmful. Most people are right handed, which also plays an important role with the person in seat C, so it behooves a leader to pay attention to whom is on their right and whom is on their left, at minimum.

Traditional office politics often disregard all that we now know about seating and tends to place the second in command in seat C and the "up-and-comer" in the company to the left or in seat D. Additionally, research shows that when there is a strong leader, members of the meeting will direct their comments to the person adjacent the leader, mostly the person in seat C, because it avoids direct eye contact and confrontation with the leader. While this is not always the case, perception, in this instance plays a vital role.

As the leader of the meeting, it benefits you to understand these meeting dynamics because you can determine who will sit in these locations. Think about the desired results you want to achieve in your meeting and then make your selections wisely. It can have a powerful impact on the conclusion of the meeting or presentation.

Positions E or F: Middle

The middle positions can be utilized for a few different purposes. The middle seats have less eye contact with those in the meeting, and direct eye contact with the leader is more difficult. The people in these seats are often talked over and around. If you want your opinion and views heard, you will need to lean forward and/or raise your hand slightly to gain eye contact and the attention of the leader to make your statement.

The middle positions are often selected by those who support collaboration among the members. One is surrounded by others, and it is easier to agree and comment with those close to you; therefore, the middle position is non-threatening. You send the message that you are approachable and part of the team. These positions can also help to soften or mitigate individuals with opposing viewpoints, especially when you are sitting right next to them on the same side of the table.

Sit in one of these seats if you're not concerned with being heard and/or if you prefer to observe. If you are unfamiliar with the group, these middle positions are effective for assessing the members and agenda of the meeting without worrying about being called upon; and especially effective when you're not concerned with making direct eye contact with the meeting leader.

Sitting in the middle of the table as the leader will encourage more interaction among the participants

---

If you are the leader, you can change the dynamics of the meeting if you sit in one of these positions. Depending upon your desired result, sitting in either of the middle positions of the table (E or F) as the leader will encourage more interaction among the participants, because you are now sitting with them. It creates a collaborative environment in which the participants will be more likely to share their thoughts and ideas. Keep in mind that you won't have direct eye contact with everyone; this can be advantageous if you have members or employees who don't typically speak up and share when direct eye contact is a factor. If you decide to sit in this location, you can strategically place people at either the end of the table (seats A and B) who you wish would share more with the group. Especially if they are more introverted, members of the meeting will feel more comfortable to open up and share their opinion when seated in the powerful position.

You will see this middle-seat arrangement used often at weddings and other important events, where the bride and groom or person of honor is seated in the middle position(s) of the table. The next most important guests will surround them to their immediate right or left. One famous example of this is depicted in *The Last Supper* by Leonardo Da Vinci. In the painting, Jesus is seated in the middle of a long rectangle-shaped table, and the disciples next to him are his most steadfast supporters.

Another example that demonstrates strategic middle-seating is in the cabinet meetings of the President of the United States.

The seating arrangement reflects the relative importance of each cabinet member. The Vice President sits opposite the President, which is the second highest position in the center of the table in this situation. The Secretary of State, ranking first among the department heads sits on the President's right, which is the most influential and supported position to the President. The Secretary of the Treasury, ranking second, sits to the Vice President's right, which is the most influential position to the Vice President. The Secretary of Defense, ranking third, sits to the President's left, which is the second most influential to the President. The Attorney General, ranking fourth, sits to the Vice President's left, which is the second highest to the Vice President. Most likely this arrangement began more out of practicality so that the President could hear the members better and they could hear the President. The table is 40 feet long, so distance does play a role in the dynamics of this meeting.

Positions G or H:

If the leader is in seat A, then these positions are the farthest from the leader, and they will have difficulty being heard. The leader will have difficulty making direct eye contact with them. If they wish to be heard, they will need to speak up and/or raise their hand to get the leader's attention. Otherwise, if they prefer not to participate, one of these seats would be a good choice.

Depending upon who is in position B, positions G and H can be used for different strategies. Just as the positions C and D support the leader (position A), positions G and H can support the person seated in seat B. If you know there will be opposing views presented to the leader by the person in position B, then you can provide a unified front with this person by sitting in either position G or H, thereby persuading other members of the meeting to see the opposing point of view.

If you know you will need to leave the meeting early, selecting seat G will allow you to leave with minimum disturbance. Keep in mind that if you have an important part in the agenda or you have valuable input to add to the meeting, you will want to choose another location in order to have the advantage of your opinion being heard before you early exit.

Seats along the wall, not at the table:

When seats are positioned along the wall to provide additional seating in the room, these are referred to as the gallery seats. These are most common for people who should hear the items discussed in the meeting, although participation is not expected. These people won't be an integral part of the meeting. These seats can also be used for administration positions, where the admin employee is required to take notes and provide information if needed. If you know you will need to leave a meeting early, one of these seats would be a good alternative to seats G/H.

Some companies will also place additional chairs along the wall to provide more room around the table while also allowing easy access to extra chairs when a meeting will utilize all the chairs available. Keeping them along the wall makes it easy to pull them up to the table so that each person has a seat at the table. While each member will be close to one another in proximity (good for inclusion and collaboration), this arrangement isn't ideal because it is not that comfortable. Unless inclusion is important, the rule of thumb here is "less is more".

Dynamics of a Round Table:

As you may recall from the previous chapter, King Arthur and the Knights of the Round Table is the best-known round table.

The intent behind the use of a round table was equal status around the table, and there would be no true head. Because of the large size of the table, about 18 feet in diameter, power positions did occur. Those who were in closest proximity to the king revealed the highest ranks among the knights and most likely his strongest supporters. The person who sat opposite the king could be seen as his competitor.

We rarely see such large diameter round tables used anymore, mainly due to the lack of space needed to accommodate a large table. Round tables are mostly used for smaller meetings. When two to four people gather for a meeting, the round table provides equal status, good eye contact to each member, and a collaborative and open environment. Depending upon the power of the leader, the positions right next to the leader will still show more power than those further away, just as in the example of King Arthur.

If you are the leader and want to encourage more collaboration and unity, you will more easily achieve this with use of a round table, if the number of participants allows for this. The more people involved in the meeting, the more likely you will need to conduct the meeting at standard board room table.

Summary:

Most meetings are a bit like the beloved childhood game "musical chairs". Individuals often enter a room and sit in the closest chair he or she can find, not thinking much about it.

People select a seat closest to food, the door, choose to sit next to friends, or purposely sit away from others. Other times, people awkwardly linger around a table before taking a seat.

Until now, you may have thought that all you had to do was show up for meetings. Where you sit once you enter a room can matter just as much as the preparation you have done beforehand. Your seat strategy can have a dramatic impact on your interactions and conversational flow.

You now understand how to take the lead by choosing a seat wisely.

The information in this chapter shows how you can now make a conscious choice in your seat selection and/or influence the meeting agenda. If you are the manager or supervisor, you can use this information to learn more about the employees who attend the meetings by examining their seat selection against the information provided here. Pay attention to this in future meetings; you may be surprised by what you discover.

Although your seat selection will have impact on the meeting, keep in mind the meeting is still made up of human beings. People won't always cooperate with you, and this will be reflected by their body language and their choice of seat in relation to you. You can't control everything, although you can affect the dynamics of the meeting. The next time you are at a meeting, be aware of who's sitting where. You will start to notice the power dynamics change based on who's sitting next to whom.

Chapter Notes

Highlights of the positions:

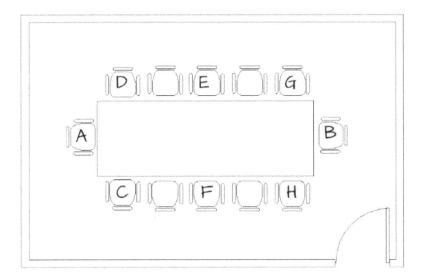

Position A: Power seat

- Leader of the meeting has best view of all members and the door with a view of who is entering the room.
- Choose this seat if you are the boss or leader of the meeting.

Position B: 2nd Highest/competitive

- Seat is at the other end of the table opposite the leader and shows second in control to the leader when supporting the views of the leader or department head.
- Often reserved for guests, this seat has easy access in and out of the meeting.
- When incongruent with leader's views, this position becomes competitive or in opposition to the leader's views.

Position C: Co-operative/right hand

- Co-operative support to the leader (A).
- Known as leader's right hand.
- 2nd highest position to leader.
- Direct eye contact with leader (A).

Position D: Supportive/up-and-comer

- 2nd highest support position to leader (A).
- Often seen as up-and-comer in a company.
- Direct eye contact with leader(A).

Positions E & F: Middle

- Cooperative to leader and all participants.
- No direct eye contact to the leader (A); therefore, gaining leader's attention is more difficult, and one will need to be assertive
- Can also be used as a leadership position and change dynamics of the meeting.

Positions G & H:

- Low status to leader (A).
- No direct eye contact to the leader (A); therefore, attracting leader's attention is more difficult, and one will need to be assertive in order to be heard and seen
- Choose this seat if you don't want to participate or be heard.
- Serve in the same capacity C and D to the person seated at B.

Chapter Four

Sales Presentations

Believe it or not, where you and your prospective client sits at a table during your presentation will play a factor in the conversational flow, success in closing the sale, and the energy in the room. Understanding the information covered in this chapter will enable you to set up every meeting for success, even before you begin presenting.

You can have your presentation planned perfectly, at least in your mind, and then unexpected circumstances happen either before or during your presentation. Perhaps your prospect invites someone else to the meeting you weren't expecting, or the space you need to meet in has a less-than-ideal layout, or any other number of issues that might arise.

This is what can make the profession of sales exciting in one way and frustrating in another. I mention this because whether you are just starting out in sales or a sales veteran, anything you can do to help the sales process along toward success will benefit you.

Every sale happens between two or more individuals, and any time people are part of an equation, it can create some interesting dynamics. Sales is difficult enough as a profession; if you can increase your rapport and closing ratio with your client simply by selecting the right place to sit, then why wouldn't you apply this information?

More sales are closed when the salesperson sits to the left of their potential client than to the right

---

Research shows that more sales are closed when the salesperson sits to the left of their potential client than to the right.

I am not saying that if you sit in the right-hand seat, you will close every sale; there are too many aspects that lead to a sale for that to be true. You will still need to deliver a good presentation, but I am suggesting that by simply understanding seating strategy, you can increase the percentage of your successful closes.

Keep in mind that I am not talking about manipulating people in any sales presentation. What we're discussing is basic human nature and information you can use to have your meetings and presentations proceed with more success.

In this chapter we will look at various situations you will encounter in your sales presentations. Whenever possible, you will want to be the one deciding where each person sits, instead of leaving it to chance. Choosing who sits where is not always possible, but you can still make some minor changes or modifications to benefit you during your presentation. We will look at each position you will encounter and understand the purpose and rationale of each.

You will notice that this information relates directly to what we covered in the previous chapter regarding conference room meetings. Here, we will look at each seating arrangement in more detail to understand how it applies in more intimate meetings with two to three people.

Corner Position:

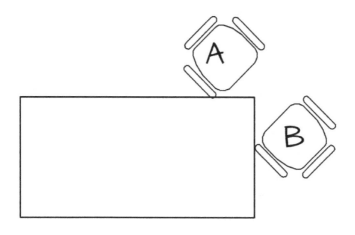

Diagram 11

The corner position seating arrangement creates a casual, friendly environment for conversation. It has an advantage over having a confrontational "face to face" setting, which can be perceived as too direct and aggressive – not the most welcoming qualities to display when you are meeting someone new or presenting to a prospective client.

Corner positioning allows for good eye contact and the opportunity to use numerous hand gestures and body language expressions as well as, a vantage point to observe the gestures of the other person. The corner of the table or desk is a partial barrier for each person, which is important because it will provide some security if one person begins to feel threatened for any reason, and at the same time avoids territorial division of the table or desk.

This is the most successful strategic position from which you, the salesperson in position B, can deliver a presentation to your prospective prospect in seat A. By simply occupying the chair in location B shown in the above diagram, you can prevent a tense atmosphere and increase the chances of a positive outcome.

You will also notice in this diagram that the chairs are positioned at a 45-degree angle. This allows for direct eye contact between both parties. The meeting may begin with the chairs facing the table directly or at perpendicular angles to the table, which creates a more formal conversational environment. If the meeting begins this way, after a few minutes and when you sense the conversation is becoming more relaxed, simply move your chair to be at a 45-degree angle to the table. The other person will most likely mirror you and turn his or her chair. If the other person doesn't turn his or her chair, you will still want to stay in the 45-degree angled position because this presents you as less competitive and more cooperative. This position also allows independent thoughts and ideas of both parties to flow because the proximity permits intimacy in the conversation.

Another dynamic of this seating arrangement is helpful for a few reasons as it relates to times when we need to recall information. During recall, we tend to look up, which triggers memories and information in our brains. We also naturally tend to look away periodically in any conversation. And sometimes we *need* to look away because the conversation may be a bit uncomfortable and looking away often relieves pressure during the interaction. No matter the reason one feels the need to look away, this position creates a safe, casual setting in which by allowing each person the option to easily avert eye contact to somewhere else in the room while the other person is talking.

The other significant thing to keep in mind with the corner seating arrangement is to sit to the left of your prospective client whenever possible, especially if you'll be giving a presentation. Research shows that more sales are closed when sitting to the left of your client. This is because you are speaking more into the right brain hemisphere of your client, which is the emotional side, and where we all make most of our decisions. (We make decisions based on emotions and then justify them logically.)

Cooperative Position:

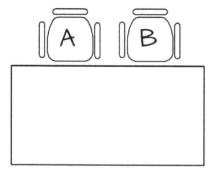

Diagram 12

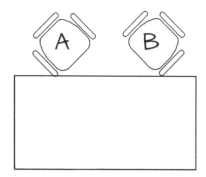

Diagram 13

The cooperative position provides the best situation when both parties will need to cooperate on a project or topic together. Both parties will find it easier and more natural to work together because it creates a natural environment of collaboration and teamwork. When you are sitting beside someone, it naturally adds a cooperative spirit to the conversation.

This position automatically creates a feeling of mutual interest and effort. It helps to establish a more intimate bond between the two parties, and you will tend to look at things from the same perspective. You are physically working together on the same side, from the same position.

There are two possible chair arrangements for this position, each one helps to create a different level of connectivity and interaction between the two people. In Diagram 12, the chairs are facing the table directly or perpendicular to the table. This orientation shows that there is cooperation between the two people. It is not ideal because eye contact between the two people is awkward, which decreases the level of sharing. This position is mostly used when two people are discussing a topic with other members of the team opposite the table. If this is the situation, keep in mind that this will have team members in a competitive position, which may have one team against the other.

The second modification of this position is shown in Diagram 13. You will notice that the chairs are turned at a 45-degree angle toward each other. This arrangement is more intimate because there is no barrier to interfere with the sharing of information. This is the ideal position when both parties are working on a common goal or project.

This position will require some trust and intimacy to exist before it can be used effectively. You don't want to start in this position if you have not met the person before. An example of this situation is when you are in a public space and another stranger sits right next to you and begins talking. Your personal space is invaded, and you quickly put up emotional barriers and resistance.

This is not the first position you want to take if you are presenting to a prospect for the first time. You will first need to test the circumstances before moving into this position. You can begin at the corner position and then ask if you can move into the cooperative position. If your prospect agrees, then you are on a good path to a cooperative meeting. This doesn't assure you that you will become their best friend just by sitting next to them, nevertheless, it will create the best situation for the conversation to progress toward trust and partnership.

When you are meeting in this position, you now become the consultant to your prospect or client instead of sitting across the table, which can create a perceived atmosphere of the "us-vs-them" scenario. This position is less formal than the competitive position as well, so if your goal is more cooperation, this position will serve you well.

When you are invited to sit in this position by your prospective client, they are telling you they feel comfortable with you and feel a level of trust. When you are not invited to sit next to them in this position, you will want to test the situation first before automatically sitting in this position.

Each of us has our own personal space bubble, and when someone invades our "bubble," we become uncomfortable especially if we didn't make the first move. So, test it out using the aforementioned "corner seating" tactic to see whether or not this position will work for the situation.

While the corner position is good for presenting, the cooperative position is also good for this purpose because you will find it easier to achieve agreement and collaboration with the other person -- this is especially important in a sales presentation.

Here's another scenario: if you are in the prospective client's office and are presenting across from his or her desk, you can test to see if you can come around to their side to show them the information. For example, you may want to show them something on the computer or if you have a brochure or other document, it is always your best move to ask if you can show them the information when you are next to them instead of across from them.

Another tactic you can use to ease the situation, so it doesn't feel uncomfortable, is to have something in-between the both of you, so it feels like a barrier in a sense. You can have a notepad for instance, or a computer works well, too. Now with all the technical tools we have available, if you have your presentation or information on a device, you will be able to readily utilize this positioning because you and your client will both need to see the information at the same time.

Introduction of a 3rd person:

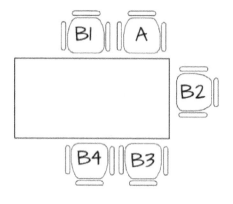

Diagram 14

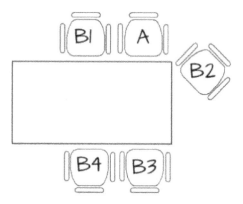

Diagram 15

You may find yourself meeting with your prospect, and for one reason or another, a third party needs to join the meeting. This often occurs in business meetings if you are presenting to your direct contact, and he or she needs to bring someone else from their company in either to review the information or answer questions. Or perhaps this third person might be the final decision maker.

Regardless of the reason behind the third party's attendance, you want to maintain control of the situation and present a positive and cooperative front to the new party as well. You can utilize the seating arrangement in Diagram 14 to help you do this. As you see in the diagram, if your prospective client is seated at A, and the third party is seated at either positions B3 or B4, the best location for you will be in seat B1. In this location you become an ally for your prospect, as the two of you are in the cooperative position, so you appear as a united front to the third party. This works especially well if the third party is from outside the company.

For example, if I am the designer in a meeting with a client and a construction contractor (third party) attends the meeting, I can easily support the desired goal of my client by sitting in seat B1. Together, this positioning allows myself and my client to present a united front ensuring the design and details remain as discussed, should the contractor attempt to steer the project in a different (and undesired) direction.

You will also be able to ask questions on behalf of your client to the third party, which shows a cohesive front between you and your client. In a situation like this, the meeting will usually produce more favorable results for you and your client.

The second-best location for you would be in seat B2, the corner position. You are still close to your prospect so you can easily support them, and you also will not appear confrontational to the third party. Moving your chair closer to your client than the third party also shows support. Another way to position your chair is at the angle shown in Diagram 15. Doing so presents a more cooperative atmosphere to the third party.

Competitive Position:

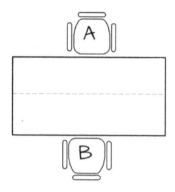

Diagram 16

When you sit directly across from someone either at a table or desk, it creates a defensive, competitive atmosphere that can lead to each person taking a firm stand on his or her point of view. The meeting or conversation can quickly become another "us-vs-them" encounter. The desk or table serves as a large barrier, helping each person to feel protected behind it.

When we are shielded (in this instance by the table or desk), we don't easily change our opinion or allow our defenses to go down. The line down the center represents the territory created by each person. We naturally declare what is our side of the table.

Many business meetings tend to start out in this position, especially if it is in your client's office and they are sitting behind their desk, and the only place you can sit is in one of the guest chairs in front of the desk. Your goal is to persuade or sell the other person on your product or service, and this arrangement will not serve you best. If the meeting takes place at a table, you now know to select a seat in either the corner or cooperative position. When it is a desk, it is more difficult to do so, and the person behind the desk is declaring that he or she is in their private territory.

Throughout my career, I have installed a lot of furniture in offices where the desk is situated with the person who occupied the office seated behind the desk facing the door and the guest chairs are right in front. Various research studies show that the manager or supervisor who has this type of layout in their office is perceived as more authoritative. This works well when the person desires to project this image. Some may also want to protect their status in the company, and this arrangement supports it. When a manager discusses issues with an employee, especially if he or she needs to reprimand the employee, this position works well.

When the desk is turned in such a way as to not create a barrier (against the wall for example), it creates a cooperative atmosphere, and research shows that these managers are perceived as more open-minded and fairer in listening to others' ideas without criticism or favoritism.

Another interesting research study was conducted by psychologist Richard Zweigenhaft of Guilford College in North Carolina, where he found that the faculty who used their desk as a barrier were rated to have poor interaction with students, and they were also rated less positively than faculty who did not use their desk as a barrier.

Another experiment conducted in doctor's offices by a research firm showed that the presence or absence of a desk had a significant effect on whether the patient was relaxed and comfortable or not. When a desk was present and they sat in this competitive position, only 10 percent of the patients felt at ease. The percentage increased to 55 percent when the barrier or desk was removed.

The competitive position will also have direct influence on your negotiations. If you are person B (Diagram 15) and want to persuade person A, this position will reduce your success ratio because of the defensive/competitive atmosphere and perceived boundary created by the table or desk. If your intent is to reprimand the other person (for example, a manager evaluating an employee), then this position would serve you well. It will also present you as the person in the position of authority.

When you are in a sales presentation, unless it somehow supports your strategy, this competitive position will not serve you best in this situation. Successful sales presentations are dependent upon your ability to influence which is accomplished by others listening to their answers and points of view. This position does not lend itself well to the necessary open and cooperative interaction you will need to foster. Research shows that conversations in the competitive position are significantly shorter and more direct and people speak in shorter sentences. This position can also create negative energy in the meeting. Again, the corner or cooperative positions put your prospect more at ease and lead to more collaboration and agreement.

There will be occasions when it will be difficult for you to choose another position. When faced with this scenario three are a couple of strategies you can use.

- Place your chair at a 45-degree angle to the desk. This will lessen the competitiveness of the meeting because you will not be a direct face-to-face situation.

- If possible, it's best if you come around to their side of the desk to be in the cooperative position, although you will want their permission to do so. You can ask, "Do you mind if I swing my chair around over there?" Once you have permission, you have removed that boundary or virtual wall between you and your prospect.

If it is not possible for you to come around to the other side of the desk or table, you can use the following strategy to "test" the territories:

- The dotted line on the table in Diagram 16 shows the even division of the table. When two people sit directly opposite one another, both will subconsciously divide the table into two equal territories. Use one of your brochures or documents to test your prospect's territorial stance. First, place the document in the middle of the table, facing your prospect. He or she will do one of three moves: 1) lean forward and look at the document without taking it to his or her "side"; 2) take the document to his or her side; or 3) push the document back into your side or territory.

- Each move will reveal much about your prospect. If they look at the document but don't pick it up and move it to their side, the message is to stay on your side of the table during the meeting, for he or she is protecting the territory. If your prospect looks at the document and slides it back to your territory, he or she is telling you non-verbally to stay on your side.

If either of these moves happen, angle your chair or body at a 45-degree angle to the table to present because you will not gain access to move to the other side or the cooperative position.

If your prospect looks at the document, picks it up and moves it to his or her side, the non-verbal signal you are receiving is one of acceptance. Picking it up is the distinction here. This provides you the opportunity to ask permission to enter his or her territory, and you will want to move your chair to either the corner position or the cooperative position for your presentation. You will have more success in your presentation by utilizing these strategies.

Equal Positions:

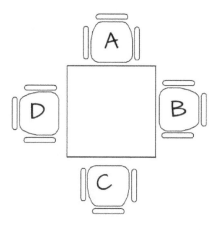

Diagram 17

When a meeting is conducted using a square table, all four positions have equal status. One person does not have a competitive advantage over another; although you should recall that you will still experience more cooperation from the person seated beside you, especially the person to your right (remember our "right-hand man"?).

If the scenario is a sales presentation and your prospect is in seat A and you are in seat B, you are in a good position, since it is the corner position. Although depending upon who else is at the table with you, you will want to be aware of some other dynamics which can occur and how it can affect the meeting outcome. If you are in seat B, and seats C and D are occupied by others who you invited to the meeting and/or are a part of your team, then you show a strong front to your prospect without him or her being too intimated by the situation. It will appear you all have equal positioning. In addition, the person from your team who sits in seat C should be someone in support of you during the presentation.

If the members are split, where seats A and B are both your prospects, and you and your team member are in seats C and D, then both teams will be more united and cooperative. This is still a great arrangement for a good outcome and collaboration between sales and prospect. This would be a more beneficial seating arrangement than if your prospects were in seats A and C, and you were in B and D. In the latter arrangement, you will create a more competitive environment because you will be sitting across from your prospect in the competitive positions. This is still a better arrangement than if you were all at a rectangular table where you are not able to all be in equal positions.

We show a square table, although it is best if a round table is available since then there are fewer barriers in the meeting because no one will have a corner position - and a round table creates an even more friendly and collaborative atmosphere. If you have a choice, select the round table as your first choice.

Involved Positioning:

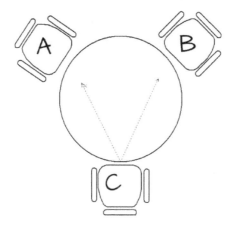

Diagram 18

If you are presenting to two people who are either with the same company or are a couple, the involved positioning will serve you best. In this illustration, you are the person in seat C, and your prospects are seated at A and B. You can see in Diagram 18 that this creates a triangular positioning. The round table creates a more informal atmosphere and removes dominant positioning. This is also good for you because you will have direct eye contact with both prospects and be able to view their body language toward you as well as one another. Prospects will reveal much in their body language and facial expressions as you are delivering your presentation. It is to your advantage to observe and take note of the signals they are sending.

This is also a great arrangement when one of your prospects is more talkative or dominant in the conversation than the other. When you find this happening, you still want to make both people feel included in the conversation.

You can achieve this by first looking at and responding to the dominant talker, followed by directing your eye contact at the quieter party, before redirecting and finishing up your answer or point with the dominant one. In this manner, you are including both parties without compromising your connection with either one. You will also find that you will gain more support from quieter persons during your presentation.

Independent Position:

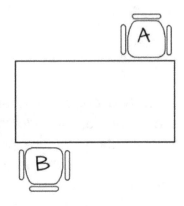

Diagram 19

The Independent position is taken when people don't plan to or want to interact with each other. It occurs mostly between strangers in public places such as a coffee shop, library, or restaurant. The message one conveys when selecting this position is lack of interest in engaging in a conversation or even indifference to hostility in some instances.

If your purpose is to show independence and you do not want to encourage conversation, this is a good position. If you desire to have an open discussion with the other person, avoid this position.

You will often observe people taking up more space than they need, creating the non-verbal message that he or she wants to be left alone. One can do this by placing their belongings such as a handbag, books, or coat on the table next to them. Be observant and respectful of this positioning when out in public.

You can also test the situation to see if you can have a conversation with them by asking a question and observing their behavior. If they answer but quickly go back to what they are doing, this is a signal they do not want to be disturbed. If the other person engages more, you can again "test" the situation by first turning your chair or body to a 45-degree angle to them, and if accepted, you can then move to a chair closer to them to have a more intimate conversation.

Summary

Where you sit during your sales presentation can set you up for success before you even begin or speak your first word. The art and science of sales is complicated enough; why not use the seating arrangement to your advantage during the presentation?

Understanding the positions and the pros and cons of each, when possible, you can preplan your meetings seating arrangements. For example, if you know that your client will most likely invite you to his or her office and you remember they have the standard competitive setup, request that you meet in a nearby conference room, preferably with a small round or square table. This will do several things. First, you will both be in neutral territory and not in the prospect's office where he or she will feel more dominant. Second, your client will be more focused on you and your presentation and be away from the phone ringing and other interruptions. And third, you can position yourself and your client in the best seating for a successful outcome.

Chapter Notes:

Corner position:

- Creates a casual, friendly environment for conversation
- Non-confrontational
- Allows for good eye contact and hand gestures for both parties
- One of the best positions to present to your prospect

Cooperative position:

- Creates collaboration between parties
- You are more consultative with your prospect
- Establishes a bond between both parties
- Ideal position for a sales presentation

3rd person:

- Positions your to be your prospect's ally in the meeting
- Strategic position to create more cooperation in the meeting

Competitive:

- Creates a formal, more competitive environment
- Can be viewed as confrontational
- Test the situation by asking if you can move to their side; if yes, do so
- Test the territory by using a document to discover if your prospect is open or not

Independent:

- Conveys lack of interest
- Use if you don't want to converse with another person (s) at the table.
- Don't use for sales presentations

Chapter Five

Large Audience Meetings

When you enter a large meeting space or event, do you just take the first seat you see available? Or do you strategize on which is the best location? Or perhaps you don't think about where your seat is located and just look to sit with someone you know.

Most of us have an internal agenda and select our seat accordingly.

Where you sit in the audience will influence your attention level, motivation, and retention of the information presented. In addition, where you sit will, in turn, influence the speaker or presenter.

You may not have thought about where you sit in these terms before. In this chapter we will discuss furniture layouts, the dynamics of the room from both the presenter's and audience's point of view. Just as we discussed the dynamics of conference rooms and sales presentations in previous chapters, large meetings and events also create specific environmental dynamics.

Layout/Set Up

The layout of the room for any large group will have an impact on the message presented by the speaker as well as on the audience. When you are the speaker, it is important to know the main purpose of your presentation and, whenever possible, to arrange the tables and chairs to support your purpose.

Consider the following before you select a venue or meeting room:

- Do you want audience participation during your presentation, training, or speech?
- Do you want to entertain or inform the audience?
- Will it be necessary for the audience to be able to take notes during your presentation?
- Will you need a monitor or screen to present slides or information?
- Is it important for audience members to clearly see you at all times?
- Do you want to create a collaborative atmosphere between you and the audience?

Your answers will help you determine the type of venue to select and/or how you prefer the seating to be arranged. Once you get clear on the purpose, you can choose the best furniture layout for the room. Let's review the various seating arrangement options and the dynamic aspects of each.

Theater Seating:

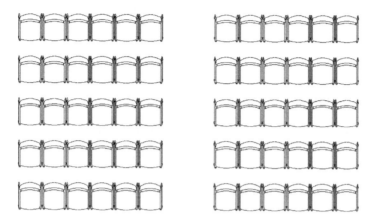

Front of Room

Diagram 20

Theater seating is the most common and simplest layout found at many events. We also see this in theaters, whether for a live production or a movie. This layout is characterized by individual seating, all facing the front or main stage. The size of the room and seating capacity will determine if there is a center aisle or not.

Advantages:

- All seats face toward the front of the room.
- Maximum seating capacity is achieved.
- Layout is best if you are presenting in a lecture format or presentation where you desire minimal audience participation.

Disadvantages:

- Audience participation is at minimum.
- The people on the end of each row or the sides will have difficulty seeing the monitor or screen.

- The audience is closed in so that if one needs to leave, they will need to interrupt the meeting, pushing or moving in front of others.
- Audience interaction with one another is low or hindered because members are not facing each other.

Common usage for meetings:

- General meetings, such as company annual meetings, where the purpose is to inform without audience participation
- Lecture format where everyone is facing the speaker
- Typical events where maximizing the seating capacity is important

If your purpose is to inform and educate the audience with your presentation and information, and does not require much audience participation, this is a popular layout.

Classroom:

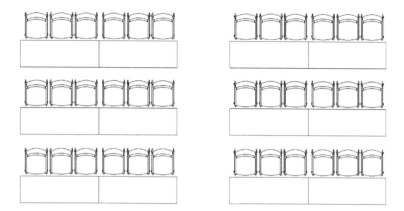

Front of Room

Diagram 21

This is the standard layout you will find in schools and lecture halls, with the chairs and tables aligned in straight, consecutive rows.

Advantages:

- All seats are facing toward the front of the room.
- The tables provide a surface for people to take notes during your presentation.
- Promotes cooperation

Disadvantages:

- Audience participation is at minimum, since they are positioned in the theater style.
- The people on the end of each row or the sides may have difficulty seeing the monitor or screen.
- The audience is closed in so that if one needs to leave, they will need to interrupt the meeting, pushing or moving in front of others.

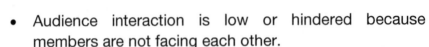

- Audience interaction is low or hindered because members are not facing each other.
- Larger aisles are required to provide room for the chairs behind the tables as well as leaving space for one to walk behind, thus reducing the space's overall capacity.
- Seating capacity is reduced for the space because of the extra space needed for the tables.

Common usage for meetings:

- Classroom instruction or training when the audience will need to take notes
- Lecture format where everyone is facing the speaker

This layout is best utilized when the information you are presenting requires audience interaction in learning the material, especially when a surface is needed for note taking or additional presentation materials such as literature. This is also a good layout if the audience will be using a computer or other device to take notes or view your information.

Herringbone:

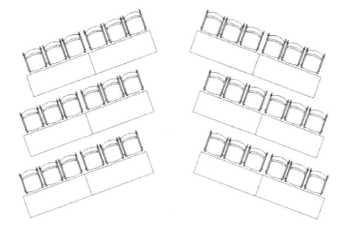

Front of Room

Diagram 22

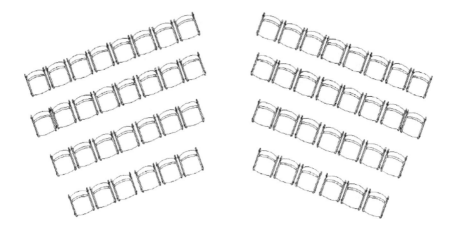

Front of Room

Diagram 23

These Herringbone layouts are modifications of the classroom layout (Diagram 22) and the theater layout (Diagram 23). The rows are angled inward toward center of the room while facing the front of the room.

This layout provides direct and clear viewing of the front of the room, so the people sitting on the ends of each row can easily see the stage or screen. A center aisle is provided to allow for easy entrance and exit and allows the speaker to approach the audience members.

Advantages:

- All seats are angled facing toward the front of the room, providing the audience members a clear view of the front without having to turn one's head to look toward the front.
- When tables are used, it allows for note taking.
- A center aisle is created, allowing for easy access and space for the speaker to interact with the audience.

Disadvantages:

- Audience interaction is at minimum, since they are not facing one another.
- The audience is closed in so that if one needs to leave, they will need to interrupt the meeting, pushing or moving in front of others, even with a center aisle.
- Larger aisles are required if tables are used to provide room for the chairs and tables as well as space for one to walk behind.

Common usage for meetings:

- Classroom instruction or training
- Lecture format where everyone is facing the speaker
- Large events and meetings

This layout is best utilized when you are presenting before a larger audience, and it is important for them to easily see you and your screen or monitor if you have one. It will also allow you to interact with the audience more easily as you walk down the center aisle.

One note about this layout is that in most rooms or spaces, setting up the room in this format will not reduce the seating capacity of the room. At first glance, one would think it would, although in most circumstances it doesn't. You may have a couple of shorter rows in the back or front, which will not take away from the overall layout. When possible, this is your preferred layout over standard classroom or theater.

U-Shape:

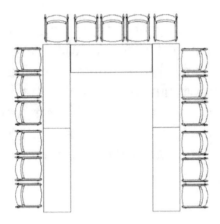

Front of Room

Diagram 24

As the name suggests, this layout is in the shape of the letter U, with tables and chairs arranged in an open-ended configuration with the audience members facing inward toward one another. You may recall that we discussed the U-shape layout in detail in Chapter 2 (on page 22).

Advantages:

- Audience interaction is enhanced, which creates open conversations and collaboration.
- The tables allow for note taking.
- Everyone is facing the presenter.
- Presenter can easily approach and engage with the audience.
- There is easy entrance and exit access for audience.

Disadvantages:

- It's an inefficient use of floor space with seating capacity reduced.
- Most members are seated side by side, and some may have difficulty viewing the presentation screen.

Common usage for meetings:

- Classroom instruction, training, or workshops
- Trainings where more audience participation is required
- Large conference meetings

Horse Shoe Shape:

Diagram 25

The Horse Shoe shape is a modification of the U-shape layout. This layout is typically arranged without tables so that the arrangement is more curved like a horse shoe. The audience all face inward with one open end.

Advantages:

- Audience interaction is enhanced, which creates open conversations and collaboration.
- Everyone is facing the presenter.
- Presenter can easily approach and engage with the audience.
- There is easy entrance and exit access for audience.

Disadvantages:

- This is an inefficient use of floor space with seating capacity reduced.
- Note taking is difficult with no tables.

- Most members are seated side by side, and some may have difficulty viewing the presentation screen. (Though the layout can be widened to prevent this.)

Common usage for meetings:

- Classroom instruction, training, or workshops
- Trainings where more audience participation is required
- Large conference meetings and team meetings

Hollow Square:

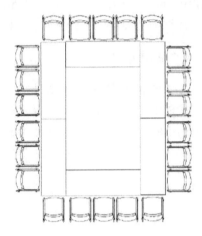

Diagram 26

This layout is similar to the U-Shape; however, there is no open end. The audience members are all facing one another.

Advantages:

- Audience interaction is enhanced, which creates open conversations and collaboration.
- The tables allow for note taking.
- There is easy entrance and exit access for audience.

Disadvantages:

- It's an inefficient use of floor space with seating capacity reduced.
- There is no main presentation area or front of room.

Common usage for meetings:

- Layout works well when participation or interaction is desired among all audience members. Works well for discussions.
- Large conference meetings

This layout works well if the leader prefers to not have a dominant leadership style and prefers to encourage discussion within the group. No matter where the leader or speaker sits, he or she is part of the group.

Banquet:

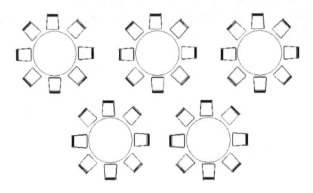

Diagram 27

Large round tables are used in the banquet style layout. This layout is used mostly for events where food is served and it's good for discussion among members of the same table.

Advantages:

- Audience interaction is enhanced with open conversations and collaboration at each table.
- The tables allow for note taking and dining.
- Name placards at each setting are often used, resulting in easy-to-control seating assignments

Disadvantages:

- It does not maximize the use of the space with the tables and chairs.
- There will be some participants at each table who will have their backs to the presentation or front of room and will need to turn their chair to see.
- Movement throughout the space can be difficult, depending upon how close the tables are to one another.
- This layout creates individual, closed, small groups per table.

Common usage for meetings:

- Gala dinners and award nights
- Wedding receptions and dinners
- Presentation events where food is served during presentation

This layout works well when your training or presentation requires the audience to work in teams when reviewing the material. It can also provide the leader more ability to move around the room to answer questions and assist with questions during the exercises.

Cabaret:

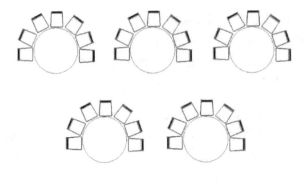

Stage

Diagram 28

This is similar to the banquet style; however, by seating the audience in an arc shape around the table with all members facing in one direction, you establish the stage area or front of the room.

Advantages:

- Audience interaction is enhanced with open conversations and collaboration at each table.
- The tables allow for note taking and dining.
- Name placards at each setting are often used, resulting in easy-to-control seating assignments
- All participants face the front of the room, and no backs are toward the stage.

Disadvantages:

- It further decreases the use of the space by not utilizing the entire table space.
- Movement throughout the space can be difficult depending upon how close the tables are to one another.
- It creates individual, closed, small groups per table.

Common usage for meetings:

- Gala dinners and award nights
- Wedding receptions and dinners
- Presentation events where food is served during presentation
- Dinner theaters

Audience Dynamics - The Learning Funnel

When you are the speaker or presenter, it is helpful to understand how the audience receives and retains information.

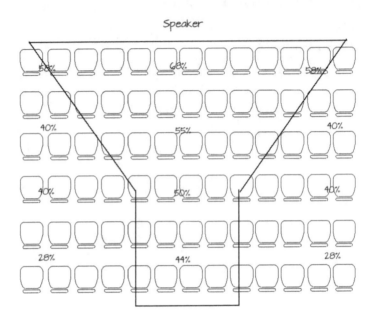

Diagram 29

A study of audiences was conducted to estimate how much audience participation took place based on seating arrangements and retention level of information presented. The results show that there is a learning or attention zone of every room, which is in shape of a funnel. (Refer to Diagram 29.)

The percentages shown on each area indicate the amount of participation, interaction with the presenter, and recall of what was discussed and presented. Those who sat in the center of the front row participated the most with the speaker and had the highest retention level. In most situations, those who chose a seat closest to the front were the most enthusiastic and motivated to learn. They also interacted with the speaker more, as their closer proximity enabled a more natural interaction.

Those seated in the center retained and participated more overall than those who sat more toward the ends of each row or the sides. Audience members seated to either side are not able to see the speaker as well as those in the center, reducing motivation and retention. The position of these audience members also makes it difficult for the speaker to see them, especially if the speaker remains center stage during his or her presentation.

The interaction and retention continue to decrease as we move toward the back of the room. Typically, those who select a seat in the back row are more negative or lack interest in the topic being discussed and prefer not to interact with the speaker or audience; it becomes easier for them to "escape" the meeting by utilizing their smart phone, day dreaming, falling asleep, or even leaving the room. Of course, there are exceptions, such as the need to sit on the end for a health reason or to leave the meeting early. In these circumstances, one would have a reason to choose a less-than-ideal seat, releasing them from the typical statistic.

Other research studies have been conducted to test this "learning funnel effect" to see if any biases explained the results such as the audience level of interest for the topic discussed, or if seat selection does in fact affect one's participation. In one study, the enthusiastic people who typically sat toward the front were relocated to the sides or back of the room. Those who sat on the sides or back row were relocated toward the front and center seats. The results showed that those who were relocated to the front and center seats had better retention and greater participation in the meeting, even though in prior meetings they were introverted or negative or showed lack of interest toward the information.

Those formerly enthusiastic people who normally sat toward the front rows and were relocated to the back rows and sides showed a decrease in participation and overall retention.

Additional research has been conducted in different classroom settings to test these overall statistics, and they all support that the "learning funnel" effect is indeed supported by seating choice. This research highlights a clear teaching strategy: if you want someone to really understand your message, place them front and center.

In another study conducted in 2004, professors Mary Benedict and John Hoag at Bowling Green State University found arranged seating affects test scores. Students who were assigned to sit toward the front of the classroom produced a net gain in test scores. For example, a student who preferred a seat in the back but was assigned to sit in a center row reduced the probability of receiving a D or F from 23 to 12 percent, for an overall gain of 11 percent. The study also suggests a lower probability of receiving an A and a higher probability for receiving a D or F for those students assigned seats from their normal middle seat choice to a seat on the side. This study is interesting because it further supports the "learning funnel effect" of an audience. The next time you enter a classroom or large meeting or event, the seat you select will have a direct effect on your learning and retention.

At some events the first row will be reserved for those who have VIP status or other important or key individuals. They are typically the best seats for the event. The next time you're at a meeting or event, notice who is sitting in the first row. If the seats are not reserved, choose a seat in the front row. If you don't typically do so, you may be surprised how it changes your view of the meeting or event.

The people who sit in the middle seats are also attentive and involved in the meeting. These seats provide a safe area because you are surrounded by others, which provides an added sense of security. Most questions and participation will come from those sitting in the middle seats and continues to increase the closer one is to the front of the room.

Audiences will naturally arrange themselves according to how Interested they are to learn

---

When you are the speaker or presenter, you can utilize this information to your advantage. If you want to impress a person, position him or her in the front row and closer to the center as it will allow you to better connect. If you know there are some you want to mute or quiet during your presentation, you can sit them at the back of the room to reduce their inclination to speak out.

The research data shows that audiences will naturally arrange themselves according to how interested they are to learn. If you like more audience participation and comments, then call on people sitting in the seats found in the main part of the "funnel" of the room layout, which results in greater success than if you reached out to those on the sides or in the back.

Depending upon your training or workshop, you could use seating assignments if you know more specifics about those in attendance. Teachers and instructors who understand the psychology of seating and learning frequently use this information to create a more effective learning environment for their students.

Your Best Side:

Researchers at the University of Oregon determined that people can retain up to three times more information about things they see in their right visual field than they do in their left. The study also suggests that as the presenter you are likely to have a better side when presenting, which is your left side. The reason for this is because you are presenting to the audience's right visual field.

Here's a deeper dive: our brains have a right and left hemisphere. The left hemisphere of the brain processes information analytically and sequentially. It focuses on the verbal and is responsible for language. It processes details to form a whole picture. The left hemisphere's functions include logic and reasoning, as well as creating strategies. The left hemisphere controls the muscles on the right side of the body.

People can retain up to three times More information about things they See in their right visual field

---

The right hemisphere of the brain processes information intuitively. It focuses on the visual and is responsible for attention. It processes from the whole picture down to details. The right hemisphere's functions include creativity, emotions, feelings, intuition, and seeing possibilities in situations. The right hemisphere controls the muscles on the left side of the body.

A research study done at the Ontario Institute for Studies in Education observed teachers and recorded where they were looking every 30 seconds for 15 minutes. The results show that teachers almost ignore the students on their right. The teachers looked straight ahead 44% of the time, to the left 39% of the time, and to their right only 17% of the time. The results also found that students who sat to the left of the teacher (<u>right side of the classroom</u>) performed better in tests than those on the right side of the teacher (<u>left side of the classroom</u>); those on the left were picked on by the teacher less than those on the right.

Parents can take note of this information and encourage their child to sit to the teacher's left side or on the right side of the classroom. This will improve the child's learning and retention of the information presented. Adults can also utilize this information when they are in a seminar or workshop to select a seat that will enhance their experience.

Stage Positioning:

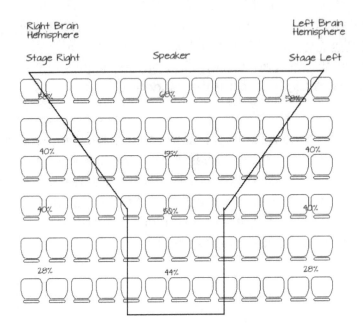

Diagram 30

When you are the speaker or presenter, you can utilize which side of the stage you speak from to reinforce your message with the audience by best utilizing the way our brains function and take in information, so you can speak to the logical or emotional side of the brain.

When you stand to the audience's left (the right side of the stage), your information will have a stronger effect on the right brain hemisphere of your audience's brain, which is the emotional side.

Standing to the audience's right (the left side of stage) impacts the audience's left-brain hemisphere, the logical side. This is one reason why an audience will laugh longer when you use humor and stand to the left side of the stage. They respond better to emotional pleas and stories when you deliver them from the right side of the stage. Most performers know that if you want to make the audience laugh you stand to the left, and to make them cry, stand to the right.

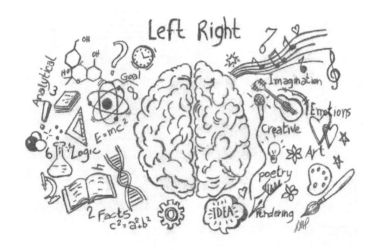

Diagram 32

Chapter Notes

Seating positions should not be accidental. Having people sit in specific locations can affect the outcome of the presentation, learning, and retention of the material.

Learning funnel

- Front rows have highest learning and retention
- Middle rows have the next highest
- Side and back rows have the lowest
- Sitting on the right side of the room provides an advantage to learning

When presenting:

- Stage right (audience's left) is best to impact the logical side of one's brain

- Stage left (audience's right) is best to impact the emotional side of one's brain

Room Layouts:

Theater: Most common layout for events

- Maximum seating capacity is achieved
- Layout is best if you are presenting in a lecture format or a presentation where you desire minimal audience participation

Classroom: Most used in educational environments and meetings

- The tables provide a surface for people to take notes during your presentation
- Standard layout for rooms although herring bone layout is better

Herringbone: Best alternative to classroom

- All seats are angled facing toward the center-front of the room
- Everyone in the audience has a clear view of the front without having to turn one's head consistently to look toward the front
- A center aisle is created, allowing for easy access as well as space for the speaker to interact with the audience

U-shape: Good option when tables are needed, and participation is desired

- Audience interaction is enhanced which creates open conversations and collaboration
- Tables allow note taking
- Everyone faces the presenter

- Presenter can easily approach and engage with the audience

Horseshoe: Commonly used for smaller group discussions

- Audience interaction is enhanced which creates open conversations and collaboration
- Everyone faces the presenter
- Presenter can easily approach and engage with the audience

Hollow Square: Commonly used for large board or group meetings

- Audience interaction is enhanced, which creates open conversations
- Easy entrance and exit access for audience

Banquet: Common for galas and meetings where food is served

- Audience interaction is enhanced with open conversations and collaboration at each table
- The tables allow for note taking and dining
- Good if small group discussions are important

Cabaret: Commonly use in dinner theaters

- Audience interaction is enhanced with open conversations and collaboration at each table
- All participants face the front of the room, with no backs to toward the stage

Chapter Six

The Private Office

For decades, the private office has been a status symbol in the business world. If you have a private office, this means you automatically have status within the company, no matter the size. The larger the office, the more important the person is within the company. Furthermore, having the corner office means you have "arrived" at your goal in most companies. As office size and one's status improves so does the quality, size, and amount of furniture contained therein. The furniture selection and choice of layout for an office can send several additional messages, such as authority, openness, inclusively, exclusivity, collaboration, formality, and casualness.

Your office furniture and layout make a non-verbal statement to those around you whether or not you're seated in your office. Showing your design or style preference is one thing; how you arrange your furniture reveals your management or leadership style. What you desire to convey to your clients, colleagues, and employees can be supported in your furniture selection and arrangements.

---

*Showing your design or style
preference is one thing; how you
arrange your furniture reveals your
management or leadership style*

In this chapter we will review the strategy and purpose of the furniture and how the layout of the furniture will influence the outcome of the work completed within the office.

Before you run out to the store or browse the Internet for furniture, you first want to answer a few questions to determine what type of furniture to purchase.

1. What are your work requirements?
   When answering this question, think about how you work and what is needed to best complete your work in the space.
   - Do you need desk space to lay out papers, or is most of your work on a computer?
   - Will you need storage for files, books, binders, supplies, and other miscellaneous items?

   Answering these questions provides you with the information you need to select the right desk unit for your office.

2. What is the image, status, or message you wish to convey?
   - Your furniture and layout reveal much before any work is done or before any words are spoken.
   - The furniture and layout create a non-verbal message to others, which can be anywhere from dictator to supporter and anything in-between.
   - Decide what leadership style you wish to convey.

3. Will you have meetings with visitors, outside vendors, and employees? If yes,
    - What is your leadership style?
    - If you want to control the meeting, then conducting the meeting behind your desk will serve your goal.
    - If you prefer to control and appear more open, you can select a desk unit that will reveal this, such as a peninsula shaped desk unit, or one that is open underneath instead of the traditional full desk.

4. Will you need a separate meeting area in your office? If so,
    - How do you like to conduct your meetings?
    - Will you need to control and lead the meetings? If so, then a table would be best. If you prefer to encourage discussion and collaboration, the shape of the table will determine this.
    - For an even more casual setting, have a loveseat and chairs with a low table.

The actual dimensions of your office will determine how much freedom you have in your selections, although don't let that limit you. There are so many options available in the contract furniture industry that being creative and designing a space that meets all your requirements can most likely be achieved.

The Desk

The desk is the main piece of furniture in any office and where most of the work will be done. Every office will have one of some style. And, of course, how you place your desk in your office sends a non-verbal message.

The area behind the desk is considered private. Facing the door with your back to the wall is the most powerful position as it allows seeing people enter.

Let's take a look at four typical office desk layouts.

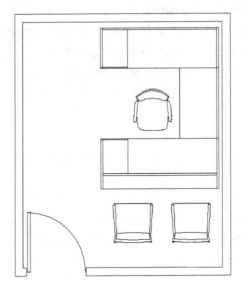

Diagram 33

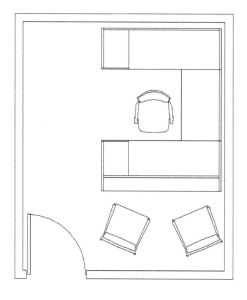

Diagram 34

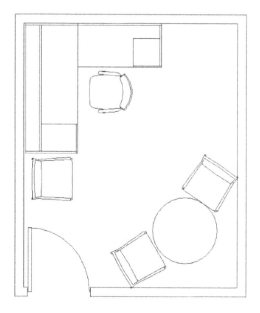

Diagram 35

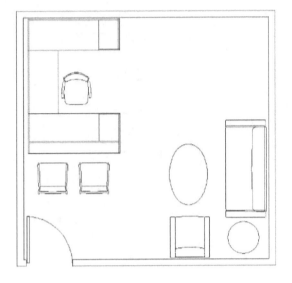

Diagram 36

The layout of the office furniture in diagram 33 is the traditional layout for an office. The guest chairs are directly in front of the desk, which provides a barrier. This layout sends the non-verbal message of authority. One needs permission or an invitation to enter your office and have a conversation, and when you give that permission, you have control.

In the layout in Diagram 34, the guest chairs are situated at a 45-degree angle to the desk; this sends a non-verbal message that you are more open and approachable, for it reflects a modified corner position. (Refer to previous chapters). This simple modification of positioning your guest chairs at an angle, is especially beneficial if you have a smaller office and don't have the room for an additional table.

The layout in Diagram 35 sends the message that you are approachable, as the chair next to your desk is inviting and shows you are open to having intimate conversations. The table is where most of your meetings will be held and this encourages collaboration and open conversations.

The furniture layout in Diagram 36 sends a couple of different messages. The desk is first seen from the door and having the chairs in front sends the same message as Diagram 33. One needs permission or an invitation to enter your office. How you position the two guest chairs in front of your desk will reveal more of your leadership style as we compared in Diagrams 33 and 34. The casual, soft seating in the office shows the non-verbal message that you also like to have more casual meetings. If you are calling on the person with this office layout and he or she invites you to the soft seating arrangement, this tells you that the person is comfortable with you and wants to have an open, more informal meeting. If you are the salesperson and presenting to this person, this is good sign that you have his or her trust.

Instead of showing several modifications of the four layouts discussed, take into consideration the following, and you will be able to easily adapt your layout to showcase your leadership style in your office.

If your goal is to quickly build friendships and foster team building, then meetings should take place without a desk, or at round or square table. You can also have a soft seating layout of loveseat and lounge chairs, or four lounge chairs and a low meeting table. Both are more informal and relaxed than holding a meeting at a table. These two arrangements are good if you like to brainstorm with your staff and others, because when we feel relaxed, our ideas flow more freely.

If you want to project power, authority and status as your non-verbal strategy or to impress potential clients and colleagues, here are some additional things you can do. Select a desk chair that has a high back, like a swivel chair on casters. Also be sure the chair is taller than any others in the room. Having visitors sit in smaller, lower-back, stationary chairs, opposite your desk, will send the message that you are in charge, and may even be a bit intimidating for some.

You can take it one step further by having your guests sit on a low sofa or loveseat across the room with a coffee table placed in front of them. Arranging your office in this manner allows you to control the space between you and others, keeping them at a distance and saying that "you won't come to them, they must come to you" - only if invited, though.

It is now becoming common to employ electronic height-adjustable desks. This is a great option and gives you the ability to sit or stand while working. There are various chairs and stools to support the various heights as well, such as "perches" that allow you to rest as you partially stand. Another advantage of having the ability to stand while you work is that when you conduct meetings and your visitors are standing as well, you will notice your meetings are shorter - something to consider if you're looking to increase your productivity and management skills.

Chapter Seven

Restaurant Meetings

There will be times when you will want to take a prospective client out to lunch or dinner to discuss business. Whether it is at a restaurant or a private club, or you have lunch brought to your place of work, all the following information applies in each circumstance.

Most likely you will be sitting at either a square or round table, unless you have a larger group where a larger rectangular table is provided.

If you are the salesperson taking a prospective client out to lunch and you goal is to close the sale or get a favorable response to a meeting, consider the following strategies and dynamics.

- Select a location where you will sit down and then place your order for food. You want to make sure you have enough time to complete your business before the food arrives, if possible. There are several reasons for this. No one makes a decision with their mouth full. Once everyone begins eating, the conversation can come to a standstill, or you may find you're doing all of the talking, rather than talking with your client. After one has eaten, the stomach takes blood away from the brain to help digestion, making it more difficult for people to think clearly. Present your proposal and information prior to the meal coming, and you won't have this issue. If alcohol is available, it is best not to partake until your business is concluded, as alcohol also dulls the brain.

- It's important to choose the right situation so your prospect or client is relaxed and comfortable, because one will make a more favorable decision when his or her defensive barriers have been lowered. The right choice in the dining environment will help in creating a relaxed, inviting atmosphere. Your prospect or client should be sitting with his or her back to a wall or barrier of some kind. Depending upon where you are dining, locations now use a variety of designs to separate spaces such as low divider walls, screens, drapes, plants, art, and even fish tanks. Having a wall or barrier behind you helps you feel more secure and relaxed. This is because you are not concerned or tense about who might come up from behind you. Research shows that respiration, heart rate, brainwave frequencies, and blood pressure rapidly increase when a person sits with his or her back to an open space, particularly where others are moving about. Tension is further increased if the person's back is towards an open door or a window at ground level.

- If your strategy is to unnerve or rattle your prospect or client to move them to a decision, then have their back to the open space or activity behind them. Depending upon your negotiations, this could be used to your advantage.

- Keep in mind that all senses will be used during the meeting. Most locations will have music playing. You want the volume to be low, so the music won't interfere with your conversation. Having to talk loudly, or worse shout, over the music won't add to a successful meeting. The type of music makes a difference as well. Music with a strong beat or music that is too upbeat, can be unnerving and create tension, instead of the relaxed atmosphere that would most benefit your meeting.

Survey the location before lunch or dinner so you can determine If It is a good location for your meeting

---

- If there are just two of you and you are seated at a square table, instead of sitting directly across from your prospective client, sitting to the right or left of them will ease the conversation and create a more intimate connection. And whenever possible, make sure you sit to their left because research shows you will have a higher chance of closing the sale.
- If you are presenting to a couple, a round table will be your best option if available. This way you will have a clear view of both your prospective clients to observe their non-verbal signals, and it is easier for direct eye contact. Remember to sit opposite both of them, creating a triangular positioning.

When possible, survey the location before your lunch or dinner so you can determine if it is a good location for your meeting. You can also discover the best table location for your meeting and make a reservation beforehand. Investing time pre-planning your meeting will place you in the winning position before you begin presenting; then the rest is up to you as to how the meeting will conclude.

Chapter Eight

Home Meeting and Dining

If you entertain at home or even conduct business at home, your home furniture plays into the success of your meetings and events.

Deciding on what table shape, size, and style for your home dining room will determine the use and atmosphere of that room. Do you desire a more formal or casual experience? Just as for conference rooms, there are a variety of table shapes available and heights as well.

To help you decide which will be best for you, answer these questions:

- How many people will need to sit around the table at one time?
- Do you want a formal or casual atmosphere?
- Will you be entertaining often, and may therefore need a sturdier or larger table?
- What is your style or design preference?
- What size table can your room/space accommodate comfortably?

The room or space you will use for dining will determine the size and shape of the table. It is best to allow at least 36 inches of space between the table and wall if possible; this allows room for one to sit at the table and for another person to pass behind them. The less walk-around space you have, the more guests will need to get "skinny" to get to his/her seat, especially if people are already seated and the guest must maneuver around them.

The shape of the room may dictate which of the table shapes will work best (rectangular, square, or round).

When deciding on the table size, a rule of thumb is to plan on a 24-inch width per person at the table; this allows room for not only the chair but also leaves space between each person.

Table options for dining:

First, you will want to determine the height of your table. There are three heights available for dining tables.

- **Standard height** of 29-30 inches. This table height utilizes a standard height chair. Standard height is comfortable as people can reach the floor with their feet. Young children will have an easier time getting in their chair.
- **Counter height** of 36 inches. This height utilizes stools with seat height around 25 inches high and is the standard height of your kitchen counter top. This height creates a more casual dining experience. The height of the stools is easier for most adults to sit in because the seat height is more at hip level. If you have young children, this will not be the best selection.
- **Bar height** of 42 inches. This height utilizes stools with seat height at 30 inches, so you also want the stool to have a foot ring or foot rest. This is the table height you most often find in bars and restaurants. This height lends to a casual dining experience, however bar height stools are not comfortable for everyone.

When deciding on the shape, refer to the chapter that discusses the various shapes for conference tables as the same applies here. The shape you select may give a clue to the power distribution in the family, assuming the dining space can accommodate a table of any shape. Rectangular tables place the parents in more authoritative roles when they sit at either ends of the table. Round tables will encourage more open conversation among family members. Square tables provide equal status for each member, which will also encourage open conversation.

As you think about your table selection, your family dynamics and parenting style should also be considered. The shape of the table will either support or diminish your authority as a parent, if that is important to you.

Where to sit:

When it comes to dining at home, we don't always get to choose where we can sit. In some families, mom and dad sit at opposite sides or ends of the dinner table. In other families, mom sits right next to dad, in the corner position. In my home growing up, it was determined early where each of us would routinely sit at every meal. We had a rectangular table. My dad sat at one end, and despite being the youngest, I sat at the other end. My mom was to my right, (which also gave her easy access to the kitchen), and my two older brothers sat on one side with their backs to the wall, on the side opposite my mom.

You may be wondering why in my family, the youngest, me, was at the end or head of the table. This was first out of necessity; it was a good location so that my mom could feed me when I was little, and my dad could help with my older brothers. As time passed, we kept the same seats out of habit. To this day, I often take a leadership role, and while I can't say for certain, I think always sitting opposite my father had a profound effect on me. If you have children, you can perform your own experiment with seating arrangements and see how it affects your family's members' personalities and dynamics.

When you have dinner parties, you can affect the conversations around the table with the similar placement guidelines for your guests.

If you want to have a specific guest feel comfortable, have them sit in a seat with their back to a solid wall. This creates a sense of security, and they will feel more relaxed.

If you have a guest whom you know is shyer and more introverted, have them sit in the power position at the head of the table. This seating position encourages them to talk more often and with more authority. It may surprise you to see that just by changing the seating arrangements, you can also influence the interactions among guests.

In previous chapters, we've discussed seating positions and how to strategically apply the information to affect your meeting outcome. Why not apply the same logic to your home entertaining? It may surprise you how the dynamics of your dinner party will change. Personally, I like to mix it up and have those who don't know one another very well sit next to each other. This encourages conversation for them to get to know each other, and it also can prevent "cliques" or small group conversations, which tend to leave new guests out of the loop. The hostess of any dinner party is responsible for the organization of the seating assignments. Use the information we've discussed throughout this book to make your next dinner event one that will be remembered for great conversation and relationship-building.

Conclusion

Taking control of your seat selection helps you achieve the goal or outcome of any meeting. Whether you are participating in a business meeting, sales meeting, social gathering, training event, or entertaining at home, you now understand why your selection of where you sit should not be accidental.

In any circumstance involving other people unpredictability is always added to the situation, although, in general, we humans tend to be more predictable in our behavior than we often realize. Our seating selections reveal much about our personality, attitude, influence, confidence, and style. The more aware we are of how this can affect the outcome of a situation, the better we can perform as sales people and leaders.

I encourage you to experiment with your seating arrangement in the next meeting you attend to test for yourself how the meeting dynamics can change. It becomes fun and intriguing to see the results, simply by choosing a different seat in the room.

To help you utilize this information at a glance, you have easy access to several single sheet guides that you reference later.

For access to your copy, go to the website to download www.sityourwaytosuccess.com/resources.

For additional information on how you can incorporate the best seating arrangement into your next presentation and further understand your audience no matter the size, visit our website - www.creativelycommunicate.com - where you will find valuable information you can use to improve your sales presentations and closing skills, communicate more confidently and effectively, and present with ease and own the stage.

Resources

Seating Capacity Chart

Table Shape	Overall dimensions	Seating capacity
Rectangular	24"x48"	4
the following shapes will	30"x48"	4
have the same seating	30"x60"	6
capacity as rectangular	30"x72"	6
BoatShape	36"x48"	6
Racetrack	36"x60"	6
Oval	36"x72"	6 to 8
	36"x96"	8 to10
	48"x72"	6 to 8
	48"x96"	8 to10
	48"x120" (10 foot)	10 to12
	48"x144" (12 foot)	12 to14
	48"x168" (14 foot)	14 to16
	48"x192" (16 foot)	16 to18
	48"x216" (18 foot)	18 to 20
	48"x240" (20 foot)	20 to 22
Square	24"x24"	2
	30"x30"	2
	36"x36"	4
	42"x42"	4
	48"x48"	4
	60"x60"	8
Round	24"D	2
	30"D	2 to 3
	36"D	4
	48"D	4
	60"D	5

Note: Standard chair is 20-22" wide, minimum allowance per chair is 24", preference is 30" allowance

References

Benedict, M. E., and J. Hoag. 2004. "Seating Location in Large Lectures: Are Seating Preferences or Location Related to Course Performance?" *Journal of Economic Education* 35 (3): 215.

Becker, F. D., R. Sommer, J. Bee, and B. Oxley. 1973. "College Classroom Ecology". Sociometry 36 (4): 514-525.

Daniel, R. 1992. "An Effect of Seating Location on Course Achievement: Comment on Brooks and Rebeta". *Environment and Behavior* 24(3): 396-399.

Danielle Jackson, Erika Engstrom and Tara Emmers-Sommer. 2007. "Think Leader, Think Male" and" Female: Sex vs. Seating Arrangement as Leadership Cues". 57 (9/10): 713-723.

Greenberg, J. 1976. "The Role of Seating Position in Group Interaction: A Review, with Applications for Group Trainers". *Group & Organization Management* 1 (3): 310-327.

Howells, L. T. and S. W. Becker. 1962. "Seating Arrangement and Leadership Emergence". *The Journal of Abnormal and Social Psychology* 64(2): 148-150.

Knapp, M. 2007, "Nonverbal Communication in Human Interaction". Cengage Learning

Lattimore, K.J. 2013. "The Effect of Seating Orientation and a Spatial Barrier on Students' Experience of Person-Centered Counseling". Cornel University

Leventhal, G. 1978, "Sex and Setting Effects on Seating Arrangement". *Journal of Psychology*. 100: 21-26.

Levine, D. W., E. C. O'neal, S. G. Garwood, and P. J. Mcdonald. 1980. "Classroom Ecology: The Effects of Seating Position on Grades and Participation". *Personality and Social Psychology Bulletin 6* (3): 409-412.

L. Morton, L & A. Mclean, M & Kershner, John. (1986). "Instructional Bias: Ignoring One Side of the Classroom". *Perceptual and Motor Skills*. 63. 639-643. 10.2466/pms.1986.63.2.639.

L Morton, L & D Wearne, T & Kershner, John & A McLean, M. (1993)." Cognitive and Neuropsychological Response Asymmetries for Adults on the Left-Right Seating Axis". *The International Journal of Neuroscience*. 72. 59-78.

Lott, D. F. and R. Sommer. 1967. "Seating Arrangements and Status". *Journal of Personality and Social Psychology 7* (1): 90-95.

McElroy, J. C., P. C. Morrow, and R. J. Ackerman. 1983." Personality and Interior Office Design: Exploring the Accuracy of Visitor Attributions". *Journal of Applied Psychology*. 68 (3): 541-544.

Mehrabian, A., Friar, J., 1969. "Encoding of Attitude by a Seated Communicator Via Posture and Position Cues". *Journal of Consulting and Clinical Psychology 33*: 330–336.

Montello, D. R. 1988. "Classroom Seating Location and Its Effect on Course Achievement, Participation, and Attitudes". *Journal of Environmental Psychology 8*(2): 149-157.

Morrow, P. C. and J. C. McElroy. 1981. "Interior Office Design and Visitor Response: A Constructive Replication". *Journal of Applied Psychology 66*(5): 646-650.

Michelini, RL, Passalacqua, R., & Cusimano, J. 1976. "Effects of Seating Arrangement on Group Participation". *Journal of Social Psychology*. 99: 179-186.

Norum, G. A., N. J. Russo, and R. Sommer. 1967. "Seating Patterns and Group Tasks". *Psychology in the Schools* 4(3): 276-280.

Pease, Barbara and Allan Pease. 2006. *The Definitive Book of Body Language* Hardcover. Bantam.

Raghubir, P. and A. Valenzuela. 2006. "Center-of-inattention: Position Biases in Decision-making". *Organizational Behavior and Human Decision Processes* 99 (1): 66-80.

Riess, M. and P. Rosenfeld. 1980. "Seating Preferences as Nonverbal Communication: A Self-presentational Analysis". *Journal of Applied Communications Research* 8(1): 22.

Sommer, R. 1967. "Classroom Ecology". *The Journal of Applied Behavioral Science* 3(4): 489-503.

Strodtbeck Fred L. and L. Harmon Hook 1961. "The Social Dimensions of a Twelve-man Jury Table". *Sociometry*. 24(4): 397-415.

Victoria L. Harms, Lisa J. O. Poon, Austen K. Smith and Lorin J. Elias 2015. "Take your seats: leftward asymmetry in classroom seating choice" *Frontiers in Human Neuroscience*, 17 August 2015

Ward, C. 1968. "Seating Arrangement and Leadership Emergence in small group Discussions". *Journal of Social Psychology*. 74 (1) 83-90

Zweigenhaft, R. L. 1976. "Personal Space in the Faculty Office: Desk Placement and the Student-Faculty Interaction". *Journal of Applied Psychology* 61 (4): 529-532.

About the Author

LeAnn Pashina is a speaker, author, salesperson and founder of Creatively Communicate, Inc. For more than 30 years she has successfully sold commercial furniture to companies in all industries. Part of her process is advising them on the design and layout of their meeting and training rooms to best meet their desired goals and purpose.

She is founder of Creatively Communicate, Inc, an expert in sales and communication skills, including how exceptional communication skills accelerate trust, build instant rapport, and positively influence decision making behavior. Her exceptional ability to communicate is the foundation of her "record-topping" sales.

Businesses and entrepreneurs alike hire her to train them on becoming outstanding in their communication and sales skills. The content of any presentation starts with understanding your audience and how to quickly assess the personality and learning styles in order to empower you to achieve your desired results. It is not only what you say but how you say it that has the bigger impact (especially on the bottom line). The way we communicate with others determines the quality of our results. Experience in training, presentations, and practice have shaped her ability to communicate with believability, genuineness and authenticity as she teaches others to do the same.

LeAnn is a member of the National Speakers Association. She is originally from Minnetonka, Minnesota where she developed her professional, pragmatic approach to design and sales by being able to communicate the "Minnesota Nice" attitude. She currently resides in Austin, Texas where she enjoys walks in the park with her loving (and slightly crazy) dog, Jasmine.

To connect, visit our website:

www.creativelycommunicate.com

Invite LeAnn for Corporate Training, or to speak at your event.

LeAnn Pashina regularly inspires audiences with her experience, passion and humor.

Her goal is to educate the audience about the importance of confident and effective communication in business, leadership and sales. She applies her experience and knowledge into action as a teacher and trainer educating the audience with creative ideas by inserting techniques and beliefs into a conventional frame work.

LeAnn is available for keynotes, seminars, corporate training. All presentations are customized for your audience, based on their specific needs. Have her present at your next conference, seminar or event.

For more information, please visit:

www.creativelycommunicate.com

or email info@creativelycommunicate.com

CPSIA information can be obtained
at www.ICGtesting.com
Printed in the USA
LVHW031805270519
619185LV00013B/691